Department of the Interior
Office of Inspector General

AUDIT REPORT

U.S. Fish and Wildlife Service
Federal Assistance Program Grants
Awarded to the State of California,
Department of Fish and Game,
From July 1, 2004, Through June 30, 2006

Report No. R-GR-FWS-0011-2007   March 2008

United States Department of the Interior

OFFICE OF INSPECTOR GENERAL
12030 Sunrise Valley Drive, Suite 230
Reston, VA 20191

March 14, 2008

AUDIT REPORT

Memorandum

To: Director
            U.S. Fish and Wildlife Service

From: Christina M. Bruner   *Christina M. Bruner*
            Director of External Audits

Subject: Audit on the U.S. Fish and Wildlife Service Federal Assistance Program Grants
            Awarded to the State of California, Department of Fish and Game From
            July 1, 2004, Through June 30, 2006 (No. R-GR-FWS-0011-2007)

This report presents the results of our audit of costs incurred by the State of California (State), Department of Fish and Game (Department), under grants awarded by the U.S. Fish and Wildlife Service (FWS). FWS provided the grants to the Department under the Federal Assistance Program for State Wildlife Restoration and Sport Fish Restoration (Federal Assistance Program). The audit included claims totaling approximately $66.2 million on 37 grants that were open during State fiscal years (SFYs)[1] 2004 and 2005, which ended June 30, 2005 and 2006, respectively (see Appendix 1). The audit also covered Department compliance with applicable laws, regulations, and FWS guidelines, including those related to the collection and use of hunting and fishing license revenues and the reporting of program income.

We found that the Department spent hunting and fishing license revenues in accordance with federal regulations, passed required assent legislation, and has adequate control over personal and real property. However, we questioned costs totaling approximately $1.4 million that were unsupported, unauthorized, or claimed under another federal award. We also found the Department had inadequate internal controls over grantee financial management, did not perform required project level accounting, and did not report all the program income earned under the grants.

We provided a draft report to FWS and the Department for a response. We summarize the Department and FWS Region 8 responses after each recommendation, as well as our comments on the responses. We list the status of each recommendation in Appendix 4.

---

[1] California uses the calendar year in which the State's fiscal year begins to designate the fiscal year; e.g., fiscal year 2004 began on July 1, 2004 and ended on June 30, 2005.

Please respond in writing to the findings and recommendations included in this report by June 12, 2008. Your response should include information on actions taken or planned, targeted completion dates, and titles of officials responsible for implementation.

If you have any questions regarding this report, please contact the audit team leader, Tim Horsma, or me at 703–487–5345.

cc: Regional Director, Region 8, U.S. Fish and Wildlife Service

Introduction

Background

The Pittman-Robertson Wildlife Restoration Act and the Dingell-Johnson Sport Fish Restoration Act (Acts)[2] established the Federal Assistance Program for State Wildlife Restoration and Sport Fish Restoration. Under the Federal Assistance Program, FWS provides grants to States to restore, conserve, manage, and enhance their sport fish and wildlife resources. The Acts and federal regulations contain provisions and principles on eligible costs and allow FWS to reimburse States up to 75 percent of the eligible costs incurred under the grants. The Acts also require that hunting and fishing license revenues be used only for the administration of the State's fish and game agency. Finally, federal regulations and FWS guidance require States to account for any income they earn using grant funds.

Objectives

Our audit objectives were to determine if the Department:

- claimed the costs incurred under Federal Assistance Program grants in accordance with the Acts and related regulations, FWS guidelines, and the grant agreements;

- used State hunting and fishing license revenues solely for fish and wildlife program activities; and

- reported and used program income in accordance with federal regulations.

Scope

Audit work included claims totaling approximately $66.2 million on 37 grants, including 12 motorboat access grants, that were open during SFYs 2004 and 2005 (see Appendix 1). We report only on conditions that existed during the audit period. We performed our audit at Department headquarters in Sacramento, CA, and visited a regional office, seven wildlife areas (WAs), and a fisheries facility (see Appendix 3). We performed this audit to supplement, not replace, the audits required by the Single Audit Act Amendment of 1996 and by Office of Management and Budget Circular A-133.

---

[2] 16 U.S.C. §§ 669 and 777, as amended, respectively.

Methodology

We performed our audit in accordance with the "Government Auditing Standards" issued by the Comptroller General of the United States. Those standards require that we plan and perform the audit to obtain sufficient, appropriate evidence to provide a reasonable basis for our findings and conclusions based on our audit objectives. We tested records and conducted auditing procedures as necessary under the circumstances. We believe that the evidence obtained from our tests and procedures provides a reasonable basis for our findings and conclusions based on our audit objectives.

Our tests and procedures included:

- examining the evidence that supports selected expenditures charged to the grants by the Department;

- reviewing transactions related to purchases, direct costs, drawdowns of reimbursements, in-kind contributions, and program income;

- interviewing Department employees to ensure that personnel costs charged to the grants were supportable;

- conducting site visits to review equipment and other property;

- determining whether the Department used hunting and fishing license revenues solely for sport fish and wildlife program purposes, and

- determining whether the State passed required legislation assenting to the provisions of the Acts.

We also identified the internal controls over transactions recorded in the labor and license fee accounting systems and tested their operation and reliability. Based on the results of initial assessments, we assigned a level of risk to these systems and selected a sample of transactions in these systems for testing. We did not project the results of the tests to the total population of recorded transactions or evaluate the economy, efficiency, or effectiveness of Department operations.

Prior Audit Coverage

On July 15, 2005, we issued "Audit Report on the U.S. Fish and Wildlife Service Federal Assistance Grants Administered by the State of California, Department of Fish and Game, from July 1, 2001, through June 30, 2003 (R-GR-FWS-0018-2003)" and "Audit Report on the U.S. Fish and Wildlife Service Federal Assistance Motorboat Access Grants Administered by the State of California, Department of Fish and Game, from July 1, 2001, through June 30, 2003 (R-GR-FWS-0003-2005)." We followed up on all recommendations in these reports and found that the Department of Interior, Office of the Assistant Secretary for Policy, Management, and Budget (PMB) considers 16 recommendations resolved but unimplemented. The corrective actions have either not been taken or documented for these recommendations. These recommendations pertain to costs claimed for unauthorized activities and accrued leave, unsupported costs, unreported program income, loss of control of land funded with Federal Assistance Program grant funds, inaccurate license certifications, inadequate controls over documentation of labor costs, and inadequate controls over equipment.

In areas where deficient conditions still existed during the audit period, we developed a finding and both repeated existing recommendations and made new recommendations. The resolution and implementation of repeat recommendations will be tracked under the resolution process for the prior audit. Accordingly, FWS should send documentation pertaining to these recommendations to PMB. The resolution and implementation of new recommendations will be tracked under the resolution process for this audit, and FWS should send relevant documentation for these recommendations to us.

We reviewed California's Comprehensive Annual Financial Report and single audit report for SFY2004. The Department's Federal Assistance Programs were not selected for compliance testing in the single audit. Further, the SFY2004 single audit report did not contain any findings that would directly impact the Department's Federal Assistance Program grants or programs under the grants.

Audit Summary

We found that the Department spent hunting and fishing license revenues in accordance with federal regulations, passed required assent legislation, and had adequate control over personal and real property. However, we identified several conditions that resulted in the findings listed below, including questioned costs totaling approximately $1.4 million. We discuss the findings in more detail in the Findings and Recommendations section.

Questioned Costs. We questioned approximately $1.4 million in costs claimed on eight grants. We questioned costs that were unsupported, unauthorized, and related to inappropriately charged payments for employee leave.

Inadequate Internal Controls Over Grantee Financial Management. The Department did not have adequate internal controls to account for Federal Assistance Program grant expenditures. As a result, the Department could not identify the composition of certain costs claimed and could not readily provide support for the costs.

Required Project Level Accounting Not Performed. Due to shortcomings in the Department's budgeting and accounting procedures, it was unable to account for grant expenditures at the project level for 12 grants that required that level of accounting.

Unreported Program Income. The Department had not reported all program income generated under eight Federal Assistance Program grants. The sources of income included activities on lands within certain wildlife areas (such as hunting-related activities and grazing), entrance fees, housing rents, and other fees.

Findings and Recommendations

A.   **Questioned Costs—$1,381,957**

1.   **Unsupported and Ineligible Matching Costs Claimed—$1,376,273**

The Department must incur both the federal share and matching State share of grant expenditures before requesting reimbursement for the federal share of grant costs. The Department, to meet its State matching requirement, used 1) expenses for salaries and operations that it paid for with non-federal funds and 2) the value of third-party in-kind (non-cash) contributions. We calculated that the Department claimed $1,835,030 of unsupported and ineligible matching costs on eight grants. We are questioning $1,376,273 in associated federal costs reimbursed to the Department ($1,835,030 times 75 percent = $1,376,273).

The Code of Federal Regulations (C.F.R.) contains multiple requirements, as outlined in the table below, which the Department did not follow in claiming its matching share of costs.

C.F.R. Reference	Requirement
2 C.F.R. § 225 (OMB Circular A-87)	Appendix A, Section C, defines allowable costs as those that are necessary and reasonable, allocable and authorized, and adequately documented. Appendix B.8.h.4 requires grantees to support the distribution of the salaries or wages of employees who work on multiple activities by documentation, such as personnel activity reports, which reflects after-the-fact distribution of the activity of each employee.
43 C.F.R. § 12.60(a)(2)	Requires each State to maintain a financial management system that permits the tracing of funds to a level of expenditures adequate to establish compliance with grant provisions.
43 C.F.R. § 12.60(b)(6)	Requires that accounting records must be supported by such documentation as time and attendance records.
43 C.F.R. § 12.64(b)(6)	Provides that costs and third party in-kind contributions must be verifiable from the records of grantees. These records must show how the value placed on third party in-kind contributions was derived. Section 12.64(c) and (d) provide guidance on the valuation of volunteer services and donated third party supplies.
50 CFR § 80.15(a)	Requires grantees to support all costs by source documents or other records that substantiate the application of funds.
50 C.F.R. § 80.16	Requires the grantee to incur costs before the grantor pays the federal share of allowable costs.

Table 1. Applicable Federal Requirements

When the Department used non-federal cash expenditures to meet the matching requirement, it used costs recorded in the accounting system that were not specifically identified with a grant. The costs generally consisted of Department supervisory and staff labor costs. The Department should have, but did not, support those costs with time sheets that have sufficient detail to determine the number of hours (and therefore the associated costs) employees spent on grant-related activities.

In addition, the Department claimed as the State match on grants W-64-D-22 and W-64-D-23 costs for permanent salaries at the Yolo Bypass WA and activities at Tehama, WA. The salaries and activities were not authorized under the grants. Additionally, the costs claimed for salaries at Yolo Bypass were not supported with sufficient time sheet detail. Finally, the Department inappropriately claimed costs as State match that were also claimed as the State matching share of costs under another federal award with the Bureau of Reclamation.

We also found that the value of in-kind contributions for which the Department provided support did not match the value of in-kind contributions claimed. The Department claimed certain goods received as the State matching share of costs based on the amount needed to support the federal share, rather than determining the amount accumulated.

We summarize in the table below the amount by which the Department fell short in meeting its State matching share of costs and the associated federal share of questioned costs. We provide additional detail on these costs in Appendix 2.

| Grant Number | Total Questioned | Nature of Questioned Costs | | | Questioned Federal Share |
		Unsupported	Unauthorized	Other Federal Award	
F-4-D-55	$239,328	X			$179,496
F-49-AE-18	73,734	X			55,301
F-49-AE-19	124,359	X	X		93,269
F-51-R-17	545,788	X	X	X	409,341
F-51-R-18	199,905	X	X	X	149,929
W-64-D-22	224,671	X	X		168,503
W-64-D-23	409,420	X	X		307,065
W-65-R-22	17,825	X			13,369
Total	$1,835,030				$1,376,273

Table 2. Questioned Costs

We reported in our prior audit that the Department had not routinely monitored its expenditures of the State matching share of grant costs. It could not ensure that it incurred and adequately documented sufficient costs or in-kind contributions prior to each drawdown (request for reimbursement) of Federal Assistance Program funds. In response to the prior audit, the Department developed procedures to record grant matching costs.

Based on our current review, the Department's policies and procedures were insufficient to ensure it maintained adequate support for all costs claimed under the grant. We found the Department adequately supported drawdowns when it claimed costs that were directly associated with a grant in the accounting system and used 25 percent of the costs to meet the State matching requirement. However, as described above, the Department generally failed to adequately support the State matching share of costs when it used either the value of in-kind contributions or salaries and operational expenses that were not directly associated with a grant in the accounting system. It generally used such expenses as the State matching share of costs in the final drawdown, when it claimed any remaining grant funds at the end of the grant period. According to a Department official, additional procedures are being considered to require additional time sheet detail that identifies work performed that is grant related.

We repeat two open recommendations from the prior audit and make one new recommendation. The Department has not yet taken action to implement this recommendation. Implementation of the repeat recommendations will be tracked under the resolution process for the prior audit report (R-GR-FWS-0018-2003).

Repeat Recommendations

We recommended in our prior audit report that FWS require the Department to:

- develop and implement policies and procedures to determine and record in its accounting system the value of in-kind services and donated goods that are claimed as the State's matching share of grant costs (Recommendation C.2. in the prior audit report); and

- establish and implement procedures to ensure that it has incurred and recorded sufficient costs and/or received in-kind services to meet matching share requirements before Federal Assistance [Program] funds are drawn down; these procedures should include the identification of specific transactions that support the amount claimed as the Department's matching share (Recommendation C.3. in the prior audit report).

New Recommendation

We recommend that FWS resolve the questioned costs of $1,376,273 by requiring the Department to provide sufficient support for the unsupported costs, claim only allowable costs, and pay back or offset any remaining questioned costs.

Department Response

Department officials concurred with the recommendation. They stated in response to the prior audit report, they developed guidelines and policies on how to identify and record in-kind and other non-federal contributions in their accounting systems. To improve the Department's performance, they will revise these guidelines to clarify the accounting processes for drawdowns and will provide training to Department staff. Officials also stated they are reviewing support documents for the grants in question. Upon completion of this review, the officials will submit to FWS a package of supporting documentation. They also indicated they plan to refund or offset under a current grant any sustained questioned costs.

FWS Response

FWS regional officials concurred with the recommendation.

OIG Comments

While FWS concurred with the recommendation and Department officials indicated they are taking action to address it, additional information is needed in the corrective action plan. The plan should include:

- specific actions taken or planned to resolve the questioned costs,

- targeted completion dates,

- titles of officials responsible for implementation, and

- verification FWS headquarters officials reviewed and approved of actions taken or planned by the Department.

2. **Costs Claimed for Accrued Leave — $5,684**

The Department charged two Federal Assistance Program grants a total of $7,579 more than the grants should have been charged for lump sum retirement and leave payouts (Grant F-51-R-18 was charged $5,568 and Grant W-64-D-23 was charged $2,011). The payouts went to three Department employees who retired or separated from State service during SFYs 2004 and 2005. The Department charged the grants the full amount of leave owed to the employees, rather than allocating to each grant only the portion of leave earned under the grant during the grant period. We are questioning the $5,684 ($7,579 times 75 percent federal share reimbursement) in associated federal costs reimbursed to the State for lump sum leave payouts charged to the two grants.

> **Example of Equitable Leave Allocation**
>
> Instead of charging the total cost for leave payouts to a single grant at the time an employee retires, the Department could charge leave costs as an expense as the leave is earned through the fringe benefit rate or some other means.

Under 2 C.F.R. § 225, Appendix A, Section C (which replaces Office and Management and Budget Circular A-87), to be allowable under federal awards, costs must be necessary, reasonable, and allocable to the federal award. In addition, the Government Accounting Standards Board Statement Number 16 states that when an employer will likely pay unused vacation leave as a cash payment if an employee retires or leaves, the employer should accrue as a liability the cost for the vacation leave as the employee earns the leave.

An official stated that prior to April 2005, the Department charged each employee's total leave payout to the Federal Assistance Program grant he or she worked on at the time of retirement or separation from State service. This official stated that due to a similar finding in the previous audit, the Department began charging leave payouts to State funds. In May 2006, the Department stopped charging State funds after it was discovered that some lump sum payments included retroactive pay and overtime. This official also stated that the Department has no way to utilize the labor system to code payments to the proper funding source.

While we understand the Department's systems have limitations, federal regulations require it to allocate leave equitably. We also note that we recommended in the prior audit that the Department resolve questioned costs associated with improper leave payout. To resolve these costs, the Department proposed revising prior grants' financial status reports (SF-269s) to include in the total outlays charging the leave payout earned under prior grant periods to those grant periods, because it did not claim enough costs to receive the full amount of federal funds available under those grants. We believe this is inappropriate because funds are required to be obligated within two years of being apportioned, and the two-year period has passed.

We repeat one open recommendation from the prior audit and make two new recommendations. The Department has not yet taken action to implement this recommendation. The implementation of the repeat recommendation will be tracked under the resolution process for the prior audit report (R-GR-FWS-0018-2003).

Repeat Recommendation

We recommended in our prior audit report that FWS require the Department to discontinue the practice of allocating leave costs to projects based on employees' pre-assigned projects [that employees worked on at the time of their separation from State service] and to establish an equitable policy and procedure to allocate leave costs to Federal Assistance Program grants and other projects (Recommendation B.2. in the prior audit report).

New Recommendations

We recommend that FWS:

1. resolve the $5,684 in questioned costs; and

2. require the Department to determine whether it made additional inequitable leave payments during the grant period, and if so, resolve associated costs.

Department Response

Department officials concurred with the recommendations. They stated that they made permanent a temporary policy they established in response to the prior audit for allocating leave costs to Federal Assistance Program grants. They are reviewing leave payments made under the current audit period to determine if additional inequitable leave payment were made.

FWS Response

FWS regional officials concurred with the recommendations.

OIG Comments

While FWS concurred with the recommendations and Department officials indicated they are taking action to address the recommendations, additional information is needed in the corrective action plan. The plan should include:

- specific actions taken or planned,

- targeted completion dates,

- titles of officials responsible for implementation, and

- verification FWS headquarters officials reviewed and approved of actions taken or planned by the Department.

B.   Inadequate Internal Controls Over Grantee Financial Management

The Department did not have adequate internal controls to account for Federal Assistance Program grant expenditures accurately. Specifically, we found that Department officials could not readily identify in their accounting system the composition of expenditures claimed on the SF-269s for certain grants, nor could they readily provide supporting documentation for the expenditures. Department officials proposed revising the affected SF-269s to correct any inaccuracies reported.

Under 43 C.F.R. § 12.60(a), Standards for financial management systems, each State must have fiscal control and accounting procedures that are sufficient to allow for the preparation of reports and permit the tracing of funds to a level of expenditure adequate to establish compliance with grant provisions. Additionally, 50 C.F.R. § 80.15(a) requires each State to support all costs with source documents or other records to substantiate the application of funds. Pursuant to 50 C.F.R. § 80.16, Federal aid payments, the grantor may pay the federal share of allowable costs only after the State incurs the costs when accomplishing approved projects. Finally, 2 C.F.R. § 225, Cost Principles for State, Local, and Indian Tribal Governments (OMB Circular A-87) specifies that allowable costs under federal awards must be necessary and reasonable, be allocable and authorized, and be adequately documented.

The problems with internal controls led the Department to inaccurately report on the SF-269s (1) total outlays; (2) the Federal and State share of net outlays, including in-kind contributions claimed as the State matching share of costs; and (3) both program income and indirect costs.

1. *Total Outlays*

   The Department budgeted for and captured grant costs using index and program cost accounts (PCAs) in its accounting system. The PCAs identify the funding source and the indexes identify the organizational unit doing the work funded by the grant. A majority of the PCAs were identified with specific grants. That is, in its accounting system, the State would label grant-related costs with PCAs designated to identify only those costs associated with an individual grant. However, the Department:

   - initially claimed the total amount approved for certain grants, rather than using the PCAs to determine the actual expenditures it could claim;

   transferred costs between PCAs in the accounting system after it had already claimed the costs, which could result in excess costs claimed under one grant that in reality belonged under another grant;

   - initially had difficulty providing a comprehensive list of PCAs by grant to support the amounts claimed;

   - provided lists that included PCAs assigned to more than one Federal Assistance Program grant and omitted relevant PCAs from the lists; and

   - recorded costs in PCAs not associated with the grants and later had difficulty identifying which of these costs were grant-related.

2. *State Matching Share of Costs*

   We identified problems with both the cash outlays and in-kind contributions the Department claimed as the State matching share of costs. We describe these deficiencies in more detail, and identify associated questioned costs, in finding A of this report.

3. *Program Income and Indirect Costs*

   We found that the Department did not include in the total grant outlays those outlays that it funded using "program" income earned from activities that are grant-related. We discuss this issue further in finding D. We also found indirect costs claimed did not match the amount of indirect costs incurred, which we calculated by multiplying the indirect cost rate by the base of direct costs recorded in the accounting system. Indirect costs are those costs, such as administrative expenses, that cannot be identified with a particular grant or project.

   According to accounting and program personnel, the Department had not developed written policies and procedures to describe the accounting processes used to control and account for Federal Assistance Program funds and other program revenues. Written policies and procedures are a critical internal control. They help to ensure that accounting procedures are applied consistently and that costs are properly authorized, incurred, recorded, and used only for grant purposes. Department officials stated that they are addressing this problem.

As a result of the deficiencies in the internal controls over the Department's grantee financial management system, FWS has no assurance that Federal Assistance Program funds reimbursed the Department were for costs already incurred, or that the reimbursement was for allowable expenses under the grants.

Recommendations

We recommend that FWS require the Department to:

1. review all SF-269s submitted to FWS for the 25 grants for SFYs 2004 and 2005, provide adequate support for expenditures claimed—including total outlays, State and federal share of outlays, program income, and indirect costs—and revise the SF-269s so they include only those grant costs for which it has adequate support; and

2. develop and implement written policies and procedures that describe the budget and accounting processes used to control, account for, and report Federal Assistance Program funding and expenditures.

Department Response

Department officials concurred with the recommendations. They stated that they will conduct a review of all SF-269s submitted to ensure that draw down amounts are fully supported. Officials indicated they follow State policies when processing accounting and budgeting documents. Based on the internal control problems we identified, we believe the Department may need additional guidance for its staff to ensure similar grant accounting problems do not occur in the future.

FWS Response

FWS regional officials concurred with the recommendations.

OIG Comments

While FWS concurred with the recommendations and Department officials indicated they are taking action to address the problems with reporting on SF-269s, additional information is needed in the corrective action plan. The plan should include:

- specific actions taken or planned,

- targeted completion dates,

- titles of officials responsible for implementation, and

- verification FWS headquarters officials reviewed and approved of actions taken or planned by the Department.

C. Required Project Level Accounting Not Performed

FWS approved funding for multiple projects under 14 grants. The grant agreements required the Department to budget and account for costs at the project level, but the Department did not comply with this requirement on 12 of the grants. We identified several problems with the Department's budgeting and accounting procedures that prevented the Department from meeting the requirement.

The requirements of 43 C.F.R. § 12.70(c) apply to each project in the grants in question because the grant agreements required project-level, rather than grant-level, accounting. For grants and projects exceeding $100,000, the regulation requires a grantee to obtain approval of the awarding agency for cumulative transfers among the separately budgeted projects. This requirement applies when the transfers exceed 10 percent of the total approved budget.

The Department's internal recordkeeping system would allow it to accumulate and track costs at the project level. However, the Department's program staff had not requested that budget and accounting staff establish unique cost accounts for each grant project. Therefore, program staff:

- budgeted for multiple grant projects using shared PCAs, rather than budgeting for each project using a unique PCA;

- failed to account for anticipated program income by project in the grants' project budgets and to report the actual use of program income by project; and

- recorded costs in established PCAs that did not differentiate among grant projects and used additional accounts, besides those identified in grant budgets, to capture and record grant costs.

As a result, the Department was unable to provide FWS with an accurate record of the total costs for each project. The FWS therefore has no assurance that funds were spent in accordance with the approved grant and project budgets.

Recommendations

We recommend that FWS require the Department to:

15

1. provide an analysis and accounting of project costs by grant for SFYs 2004 and 2005, and

2. establish a policy and implement procedures to account for and report grant costs at the project level when the grant agreements require that level of accounting.

Department Response

Department officials concurred with the recommendations. They stated that they will establish individual index and program cost accounts (PCAs) at the project level for all FWS grants, including individual PCAs for program income.

FWS Response

FWS regional officials concurred with the recommendations.

OIG Comments

While FWS concurred with the recommendations and Department officials indicated they are taking action to address them, additional information is needed in the corrective action plan. The plan should include:

- specific actions taken or planned,

- targeted completion dates,

- titles of officials responsible for implementation, and

- verification FWS headquarters officials reviewed and approved of actions taken or planned by the Department.

D. **Unreported Program Income**

Federal regulations allow grantees to earn income as a result of grant-supported activities, but require them to report and account for the income in an agreed-upon manner. The Department earned but did not report program income received or the associated expenses to FWS on the SF-269s for eight grants.

Title 43 C.F.R. § 12.65(b) defines program income as gross income a grantee receives that is "directly generated by a grant supported activity, or earned only as a result of the grant agreement during the grant period." The FWS Manual (522 FW 19.4, Exhibit 1(1)) requires grantees to report income they receive from contractor-provided services that support grant objectives on lands purchased or managed with grant funds. Titles 43 C.F.R. § 12.60(a)(2) and 50 C.F.R. § 80.15(a) also require each State to be able to track, through its financial management system, funds at a level that is adequate to demonstrate compliance with grant provisions.

The Department earned income under grants W-64-D-22 and W-64-D-23 from user fees for grazing, hunting-related activities, and employee housing rentals. The Department also entered into barter arrangements in which farmers, in exchange for use of land on the wildlife areas and in lieu of paying cash, left crops for wildlife. The value of the crops is "barter income." The cash and barter-earning activities took place on wildlife areas operated and maintained under the two grants, but the Department did not report the income earned as program income.[3]

Department officials estimated they would receive $1,643,661 in program income under grants W-64-D-22 and W-64-D-23 for activities related to wildlife habitat development and maintenance. Department officials told us that cash income was included in the projected program income amount in the grant agreements but the "barter income" was not. We could not readily identify from the accounting system or from other support how much program income the Department actually earned in cash or barter. We did, however, determine how much program income it spent for these grants. We concluded that the Department received at least as much program income as it spent. Accordingly, we believe the Department received at least $653,050 under Grant W-64-D-22 and $836,883 under Grant W-64-D-23.

The Department also failed to report program income on the following six grants. We could not determine the net effect for these grants due to lack of supporting documentation on program income received.

- On grants F-49-AE-18 and F-49-AE-19, the Department used the value of hours donated ($70,020) by volunteers who conducted tours at the Elkhorn Slough Ecological Reserve as part of its required matching share of State grant costs. As entrance fees are received from the public, we believe claiming the value of volunteer hours may require the revenue received to be reported as program income.

- On grants F-114-D-2 and F-114-D-3, the Department received rent on employee residences at trout and salmon hatcheries. The Department claimed the cost of materials used to repair the residences as the State matching share of costs, making the rental income program income.

- On grants W-58-HS-33 and W-58-HS-34, the Department earned $75,353 and $62,308, respectively; from replacement cards hunters purchased to prove they completed hunter education safety courses. While Department officials told us

---

[3] In finding A.1 we questioned costs claimed by the Department that were related to salaries and unauthorized activities at Yolo Bypass and Tehama WAs. A portion of the program income we identified that was earned under W-64-D-22 and W-64-D-23 related to these salaries and activities. Had the salaries been approved and activities been authorized, the related revenue would become program income. Whether income earned from these activities should be treated as program income will depend on FWS disposition of the recommendations in finding A.1. If they allow costs claimed for income-earning activities at Yolo and Tehama as eligible costs, associated income earned should be treated as program income. If they disallow the costs, the income earned from activities on these WAs is not program income.

they deducted this amount from net outlays reported on the SF-269s, they did not report the income as program income on the SF-269s or provide documentation to support how they accounted for the income.

Our prior audit also contained a finding on unreported program income. According to a Department official, in accordance with a policy issued in response to the prior audit recommendations, the Department included in the applications for federal assistance and grant agreements for grants W-64-D-22 and W-64-D-23 projected program income of $702,061 and $941,600, respectively. The Department official believed including estimated program income in the grant agreement was sufficient to meet program income reporting requirements.

The Department must not only project program income that will be earned, but must also account for its use on the SF-269. By understating the program income and related expenses on the SF-269s for the affected grants, the Department provided FWS no means to ensure the Department spent the program income received appropriately. Additionally, under the grant agreements and 43 C.F.R. § 12.65(g), program income received should have reduced both the federal and State share of grant costs. The Department could be reimbursed more than it should be for grant-related expenses if it fails to report all program income.

We repeat one open recommendation from the prior audit and make three new recommendations. The Department has not yet taken action to implement this recommendation. The implementation of the repeat recommendation will be tracked under the resolution process for the prior audit report (R-GR-FWS-0018-2003).

Repeat Recommendation

We recommended in our prior audit report that FWS require the Department to develop policies and implement procedures to identify and report [on the SF-269s] as program income, the value of all goods, services, improvements, or other benefits it receives from grant-related activities. This includes the value of crops or other goods and services received from farming activities on wildlife areas that are maintained and operated with Federal Assistance [Program] funds. The estimated amounts of all program income should also be included in the Department's Applications for Federal Assistance (Recommendation D.2. in the prior audit report).

New Recommendations

We recommend that FWS:

1. determine whether the Department received any excess reimbursement on grants W-64-D-22, W-64-D-23, F-49-AE-18, F-49-AE-19, F-114-D-2, F-114-D-3, W-58-HS-33, and W-58-HS-34, and if so, require the Department to return it;

2. require the Department to identify what expenses the program income received under the affected grants paid for and provide sufficient documentation to demonstrate these expenses are allowable as grant costs; and

3. require the Department to revise final SF-269s for the affected grants so they identify the program income received from grant-related activities and include in the total outlays those outlays related to program income.

Department Response

Department officials concurred with the recommendations. They stated that they developed a policy in response to the prior audit recommendation, but acknowledged they may need additional guidance. They will revise the Department's grant guidelines on the reporting of program income and accounting for all goods, services, improvements, or other benefits it receives from grant related activities. The Department also stated that it has begun a review to identify excess grant reimbursement and will submit to FWS the results of the review and supporting documentation.

FWS Response

FWS regional officials concurred with the recommendations.

OIG Comments

While FWS concurred with the recommendations and Department officials indicated they are taking action to address them, additional information is needed in the corrective action plan. The plan should include:

- specific actions taken or planned,

- targeted completion dates,

- titles of officials responsible for implementation, and

- verification FWS headquarters officials reviewed and approved of actions taken or planned by the Department.

CALIFORNIA DEPARTMENT OF FISH AND GAME
FINANCIAL SUMMARY OF REVIEW COVERAGE
JULY 1, 2004, THROUGH JUNE 30, 2006

Grant Number	Grant Amount	Claimed Costs[1]	Questioned Costs (Federal Share)		
			Unsupported	Cost Exceptions	Total
F-4-D-54	$2,308,000	$2,308,000			
F-4-D-55	2,316,000	2,504,820	$179,496		$179,496
F-6-C-53	206,000	105,575			
F-6-C-54	205,000	121,193			
F-49-AE-18	2,320,000	2,076,299	55,301		55,301
F-49-AE-19	2,287,000	2,847,161	93,269		93,269
F-50-R-17	3,003,500	3,003,500			
F-50-R-18	4,283,800	3,779,296			
F-51-R-17	6,471,000	5,761,056	205,600	$203,741	409,341
F-51-R-18	6,038,470	5,438,206	44,128	109,977	154,105
F-68-R-14	218,000	217,455			
F-68-R-15	266,000	239,359			
F-89-D-8	422,217	415,785			
F-89-D-9	404,902	358,111			
F-95-B-1	3,414,952	3,142,762			
F-97-B-1	2,353,816	2,353,816			
F-101-B-1	338,600	893,745			
F-104-B-1	278,780	271,039			
F-107-B-1	436,304	636,304			
F-108-B-1	620,496	583,557			
F-112-B-1*	1,498,976	60,000			
F-113-B-1	3,141,133	2,664,632			
F-114-D-2	3,257,000	2,827,894			
F-114-D-3	3,117,000	3,828,258			
F-115-B-1*	1,019,704	84,314			
F-116-B-1	159,016	149,238			
F-118-B-1*	230,000	0			
F-119-R-1	1,161,555	321,881			
F-120-B-1*	938,222	0			
W-29-C-58	199,760	199,760			
W-29-C-59	270,489	267,198			

CALIFORNIA DEPARTMENT OF FISH AND GAME
FINANCIAL SUMMARY OF REVIEW COVERAGE
JULY 1, 2004, THROUGH JUNE 30, 2006

Grant Number	Grant Amount	Claimed Costs[1]	Questioned Costs (Federal Share)		
			Unsupported	Cost Exceptions	Total
W-58-HS-33	1,467,500	1,481,030			
W-58-HS-34	1,467,500	1,464,809			
W-64-D-22	6,204,669	5,832,677	74,608	93,895	168,503
W-64-D-23	5,877,285	6,670,178	286,642	21,931	308,573
W-65-R-22	1,588,339	1,430,895	13,369		13,369
W-65-R-23	1,579,012	1,865,715			
TOTALS	$71,369,997	$66,205,518	$952,413	$429,544	$1,381,957

1. Represents total outlays shown on the financial status reports (SF-269).
* As the final SF-269 had not been prepared, we based the costs claimed on the amount reimbursed.

EXPLANATION BY GRANT OF QUESTIONED
COSTS RELATED TO STATE MATCHING SHARE OF COSTS

Grant Number	Questioned Amount	Nature of Questioned Costs			Questioned Federal Share	Explanatory Note
		Unsupported	Unauthorized	Other Federal Award		
F-4-D-55	$239,328	X			$179,496	a
F-49-AE-18	73,734	X			55,301	b
F-49-AE-19	124,359	X	X		93,269	c
F-51-R-17	545,788	X	X	X	409,341	d
F-51-R-18	199,905	X	X	X	149,929	e
W-64-D-22	224,671	X	X		168,503	f
W-64-D-23	409,420	X	X		307,065	g
W-65-R-22	17,825	X			13,369	h
Total	**$1,835,030**				**$1,376,273**	

a. F-4-D-55. The Department had insufficient time sheet coding detail to support $239,328 in labor costs claimed.

b. F-49-AE 18. The Department had insufficient documentation and time sheet coding detail to support $73,734 claimed. The amount included in-kind contributions for urban fisheries city/county pond management, labor for interpretive services, and operational expenses.

c. F-49-AE-19. The Department had insufficient documentation and time sheet coding detail to support $124,359 claimed. The amount included in-kind contributions for urban fisheries and interpretive services and labor for conservation education and interpretive services. In addition to the amount questioned as unsupported, the Department proposed excess matching costs (not included in the table above) that were not approved.

d. F-51-R-17. The Department claimed $545,788 in unsupported and ineligible expenses, including unsupported labor and operational costs, costs for the purchase of fish food that was not authorized under the grant, and costs claimed under another federal award (the Interagency Ecological Program with U.S. Bureau of Reclamation).

e. F-51-R-18. The Department claimed $199,905 in costs that were not supported, not approved (fish food), and related to another federal award (the Interagency Ecological Program with U.S. Bureau of Reclamation).

EXPLANATION BY GRANT OF QUESTIONED
COSTS RELATED TO STATE MATCHING SHARE OF COSTS

f. W-64-D-22. The Department claimed $224,671 in unsupported and ineligible expenses. These costs included cash outlays for (1) permanent salaries at Yolo Bypass WA and other labor costs that were not approved under the grant agreement and were not supported with enough detail in time sheet codes to tie to the grant and (2) outlays for activities at the Tehama WA that were not approved in the grant agreement. In addition to the amount questioned as unsupported, the Department proposed excess matching costs (not included in the table above) that were not approved.

g. W-64-D-23. The Department claimed $409,420 in unsupported labor and operational costs, and ineligible expenses. These costs included cash outlays for (1) permanent salaries at Yolo Bypass WA and other labor costs that were not approved under the grant agreement and were not supported with enough detail in time sheet codes to tie to the grant and (2) outlays for activities at the Tehama WA that were not approved in the grant agreement.

h. W-65-R-22. The Department claimed $17,825 in unsupported costs (no support was provided).

CALIFORNIA DEPARTMENT OF FISH AND GAME
SITES VISITED

Headquarters

Sacramento

Central Region

Fresno

Wildlife Areas

Big Sandy
Doyle
Honey Lake
Los Banos
Mendota
Pismo Lake Reserve
Volta

Fisheries Facility

La Grange

CALIFORNIA DEPARTMENT OF FISH AND GAME
STATUS OF AUDIT FINDINGS AND RECOMMENDATIONS

Recommendations	Status	Actions Required
A.1, A.2.1, A2.2, B.1, B.2, C.1, C.2, D.1, D.2, D.3	FWS management concurs with the recommendations, but additional is needed as outlined in the "Actions required" column.	Additional information is needed in the corrective action plan, including the actions taken or planned to implement the recommendations, targeted completion date(s), the title of official(s) responsible for implementation, and verification that FWS officials reviewed and approved of actions taken or planned by the State. We will refer recommendations not resolved and/or implemented at the end of 90 days (after June 12, 2008) to the Assistant Secretary for Policy, Management and Budget for resolution and/or tracking of implementation.
B.2, C.2, C.3, D.2	Repeat recommendations from our prior audit report (R-GR-FWS-0018-2003). PMB considers these recommendations resolved but unimplemented.	Provide documentation regarding the implementation of these recommendations to PMB.

Report Fraud, Waste, Abuse, and Mismanagement

Fraud, waste, and abuse in government concerns everyone: Office of Inspector General staff, Departmental employees, and the general public. We actively solicit allegations of any inefficient and wasteful practices, fraud, and abuse related to Departmental or Insular Area programs and operations. You can report allegations to us in several ways.

By Mail: U.S. Department of the Interior
Office of Inspector General
Mail Stop 5341 MIB
1849 C Street, NW
Washington, D.C. 20240

By Phone   24-Hour Toll Free   800-424-5081
Washington Metro Area   703-487-5435

By Fax   703-487-5402

By Internet   www.doioig.gov/hotline

www.ingramcontent.com/pod-product-compliance
Lightning Source LLC
Chambersburg PA
CBHW080757290526
45790CB00008B/3484